SURF

SURF

STYLE
AT HOME

RAILI CLASEN

WITH KELLI KEHLER

Gibbs Smith

To my rock, my gut check, the love of my life, Ryan. Without you, there is no one cheering me on daily. Without you, there is no one telling me I'm off track. This book, my career(s), and my life all made so beautifully because of you!

First Edition
28 27 26 25 24   5 4 3 2 1
Text © 2024 Raili Clasen
Photographs: see page 223 for continuation of this copyright page

Published by
Gibbs Smith
P.O. Box 667
Layton, Utah 84041

1.800.835.4993 orders
www.gibbs-smith.com

Designed by Part & Parcel, partandparcel.la

Printed and bound in Shenzhen, China

Gibbs Smith books are printed on either recycled, 100% post-consumer waste, FSC-certified papers or on paper produced from sustainable PEFC-certified forest/controlled wood source. Learn more at www.pefc.org.

Library of Congress Cataloging-in-Publication Data
2023940761
ISBN: 978-1-4236-6481-9

Introd

Growing up, I was obsessed with the beach. It was all I thought about from the time I woke up until I fell into bed, sandy and exhausted. I lived in landlocked Cypress, California, where I would hop on the bus, then jump on *another* bus until I arrived at the water's edge in Seal Beach, a quirky Southern California beach town. Surfers quickly became my celebrities and style icons, from hot-pink boardshorts and checkered-print slip-ons to graphic surfboards with '70s-inspired stripes. Public-beach restrooms with retro tiles, hand-painted "private beach" signs, sunny yellow short boards, colorful lifeguard flags—I was hooked.

uction

I'd come home from my beach adventures and use my bedroom as a canvas to translate the swirl of colors, typography, and patterns that was going on inside my head. I didn't grow up with a lot of money, but what I had I put toward making my room look as cool as possible. I wasn't concerned with what other people thought was "cool"; I just knew what I liked. Decorating my personal space was like adding a wink—it was all about creating a fun place to hang out where nothing was taken too seriously. If I went

to the beach, a hotel, or a restaurant and saw something that inspired me, I'd come home and reinterpret it through my own lens. Like a surfer switching boards or paddling out on a choppy day, I was always taking in my surroundings and adapting my style.

I eventually landed a marketing job at Raisins Swimwear when I was twenty-five, and after that I found my dream job at Quiksilver, where I worked for the women's surf brand, Roxy. I hooked my line onto authentic surf-culture aficionados and Quiksilver legends Randy Hild and Steve Jones, and I was exposed to a design world I never knew existed. Steve became a fast friend and a creative mentor, and I watched in wonder as he hung a Christmas tree upside down from the ceiling and dangled hula dolls from it. He helped me look at things in new ways and to see how I could make them cooler, a little more fun, and a lot more whimsical. I tagged along on photo shoots and store installations where I learned how to experiment through play. I was surrounded by innovators who kept doing things that made people say, "I've never seen anyone do that before." It was part of the culture at Quiksilver, and it fit right in with how my brain has always worked.

Somewhere in there I married a surfer and had surfer babies. Eventually the surf culture pumping in my veins collided with my desire to make my surroundings awesome. My first official interior design project was my own house. My husband, Ryan, and I had bought a new home—a California ranch—and hired an interior designer to work her magic. Well, that designer ended up moving across the country. This is the part of the story where someone else might call up another designer, but I decided to give it a whirl myself.

Since I was not a classically trained designer, I didn't have any rules to follow. I just did my own thing. My adaptability and joyous love for surf culture spilled out of me. When Ryan brought home some new surfboards from local surfboard-shaper Almond Surf Shop, I said, "These are like art! Let's mount them on the wall." When I realized I was missing a plumbing piece for our bathroom sink, leaving exposed black plastic, I wrapped all the plumbing in rope. I painted colorful '70s-inspired stripes on the wall. I dipped things in paint, turned things upside down, and colored way outside the lines. I was fearless. I used our home as a revolving door of fun and wacky ideas, and I threw them up at our walls to see what stuck. Next thing I knew, I was getting real design clients. Some of those early jobs were small and not the best, but they all had that design-with-a-wink that I put into every project to this day.

Now I'm a real interior designer with an actual office and an amazing team. Go figure! My design firm oversees projects from Newport to Montana to Baja, all of them with clients asking for that wink. After all that has transpired in my career, my takeaway is this: It doesn't cost you anything to be fearless in your home design. Surf culture is laid-back, but it is also inventive, bold, and fun. It boasts a "nothing to lose" mentality. Let's take that energy and put it into our homes, because if we do, I guarantee huge smiles all around.

The only time I push my clients to do something outside the box that they are unsure of is when I am 1,000 percent sure. And most of the time, I am 1,000 percent sure. So, let's try some stuff and see what happens. Let's be fearless with design. You've just got to trust me on this—you have nothing to lose and everything to gain from being bold.

XO
Raili

1

What the Heck Is Surf Style?

Surf style has always been more of a feeling to me than an actual style. Growing up at the beach imprinted a black-and-white-checkered, polka-dotted, striped, neon influence on my brain. But surf style is more than the brightly decked-out fashion; it was clear to me from a young age that surfing is about boldness, connection to nature, and reinvention. Surfers are creatives who really go for it and don't take themselves too seriously. When you distill that essence into a home, I bet you won't ever want to leave.

There are loads of inspiration that can be teased out of surf culture: from '70s-inspired stripes to the color explosion of the '80s and '90s surf fashion scene to early origins of beach culture steeped in washed-up rope and sun-bleached wood. Expressed on beach signage, T-shirt graphics, and vintage surf-contest posters, the surf culture and attitude evolved with one singular message: "I'm not afraid to be myself."

Combining that fearless artistry with a laid-back spirit is what surf style is all about. It's not just putting a surfboard on a wall—it's bottling that surf-culture feeling and then spraying it all over your house like a bottle of champagne being shaken by a surfer who just crushed their first big wave contest.

Working on Kelly Slater's Surf Ranch was my ultimate "pinch-me" project. I created this outdoor space to be a relaxing spot to sit in the shade with a beer and watch happy surfers ride by on perfect waves.

let the good
times roll

Surfing is *fun*. It is definitely not
a chore. In fact, someone who
goes out surfing and doesn't
catch a single wave still probably
has a big ole grin on their face
at the end of the day. Bringing
this air of happiness and fun
into the home can happen in a
billion different ways. Installing
electric-blue plumbing fixtures
in a bathroom, dipping chair legs
in yellow paint, hanging surf fins
on the wall, putting your favorite
song lyrics on display in neon—if
something makes you happy
to look at, put that thing in your
house. Don't overthink it.

sandy toes welcome

Surfers and surf culture are the opposite of stuffy. A home that reflects surf style should be a relaxing place where you can walk in barefoot and flop down on the couch without fear of messing something up. These are livable homes, not showrooms. Want to put your feet up on the coffee table? Go for it. You're not worried about sitting up straight or putting your drink on a table without a coaster. These are chill, interactive places where you can pull up a chair or a floor cushion and be yourself.

A great way to bring the outside in is to incorporate natural wood and earthy greens. Don't be afraid to mix up wood tones in your light fixtures, too.

you're a natural

Being out in the water waiting to catch a wave is like medicine to my family and so many other people who surf. This is a connection to nature like no other—you are really in tune with the outdoors. Beaches always bring up thoughts of driftwood, so surf style goes hand in hand with natural elements like wood textures and trees (because if you're on the board sitting in the lineup, your view is of the land). Blending wood, trees, rope, leather, and other organic materials will lend that nature connection to your home that is oh so important in surf culture.

bring in the waves

When my son, Wyatt, was in high school, he got a concussion playing volleyball. His doctor enlightened us about the benefits of nature on the brain's ability to heal and thrive, and he prescribed Wyatt with an hour of "green" time daily. This was meant to be time spent out in nature, with no screens or noisy distractions. For Wyatt, this really meant "blue" time, where he could be out in the water surfing. Bringing that surf feeling indoors—nature, relaxation, all of it—is good for the noggin.

Now that you have the surf report, let's get out there and have some fun.

I will show you how we can bottle up the nature connection, boldness, and reinvention of surf culture and spray it all over your house with unbridled joy. We're going to lean into what makes us smile and try something different and unexpected. We're looking for that sweet spot between weird and wow. This is your invitation to bring the carefree spirit of surf culture into your home. Once we do all of that, you will never look back.

Below: This home in Malibu, California, is not technically a house—it's a triple-wide trailer situated in a primo location in Point Dume's mobile home park. There are zippy moments (floral wallpaper, '70s-inspired stripes from the floor to the ceiling, oversized art, bold tile, and sculptural light fixtures) balanced by relaxed, beachy calm. Leave your stress at the door and put on a record.

2 Crank Up the Color

I love bursting into a room, looking for something to wow me. Think of me as a friendly critic, if you will. I'm looking for that something special that's waving its hands in the air, shouting enthusiastically, "Hello! This home is fun. This is where I want to hang, kick off my Vans, and stay awhile." It's just how my brain works—I'm always on the hunt for that little wink.

Often, spaces that are very neutral and tonal can feel, well, *boring* after a while. Yeah, I said it. But don't worry—it's pretty easy to take your space from snore to *score*! Adding a burst of color to your space through art, a stool, or a light fixture can be that something special that keeps your home feeling invigorating and inspiring on the daily. Just keep in mind: there's a time and place for that pop of color. Small spaces or accent pieces are great places to begin because they don't overwhelm; they add the perfect amount of *pop* without going overboard.

choose your own adventure

I've got good news: you're in charge of how high you crank that color dial. Think of it like swimming in a pool—maybe you just want to dip your pinky toe in the shallow end for starters. Try infusing color into your design in small doses. It can be a brightly hued pencil cup, a sunny yellow chair, a punchy pink piece of art—hello, *The Endless Summer* film poster—or a colorful light fixture. Even a whiff of color will add instant personality and contrast to whatever room you're decorating.

Or perhaps you want to cannonball into the deep end with color! You could paint your entryway piano a cheery yellow with reckless abandon. Just watch your friends' faces light up when they walk in the door.

Whatever adventure you choose, start by picking one thing—maybe it's the sofa, maybe it's a pillow, maybe it's the cup of pencils—and just practice. Bringing fun printed accessories into your all-white bathroom will change the whole vibe. Something like blue plumbing fixtures could make you smile every day. Painting your bathtub yellow is always a good idea in my book. Add color and see what it does to your space and your mood. If you're not sure where to start with color, look at art or photography and see what lights you up.

This photo of the yellow board made an impact on me the very first time I saw it years ago.

It's a reminder to me to go for those bright colors that stick in my memory and make me smile.

they call me (not so) mellow yellow

Yellow brings a big ole dose of sunshine into whatever room you're decorating. Yellow is happy. Yellow is warm. Yellow feels like the sun, and pairing the sun with anything surf is going to be a good time. Surf + sun = fun. It's my favorite color to *pop* into a room's design, but if yellow isn't singin' your kinda song, I get it. Try pink, blue, green—if it makes your heart skip a beat, bring it in.

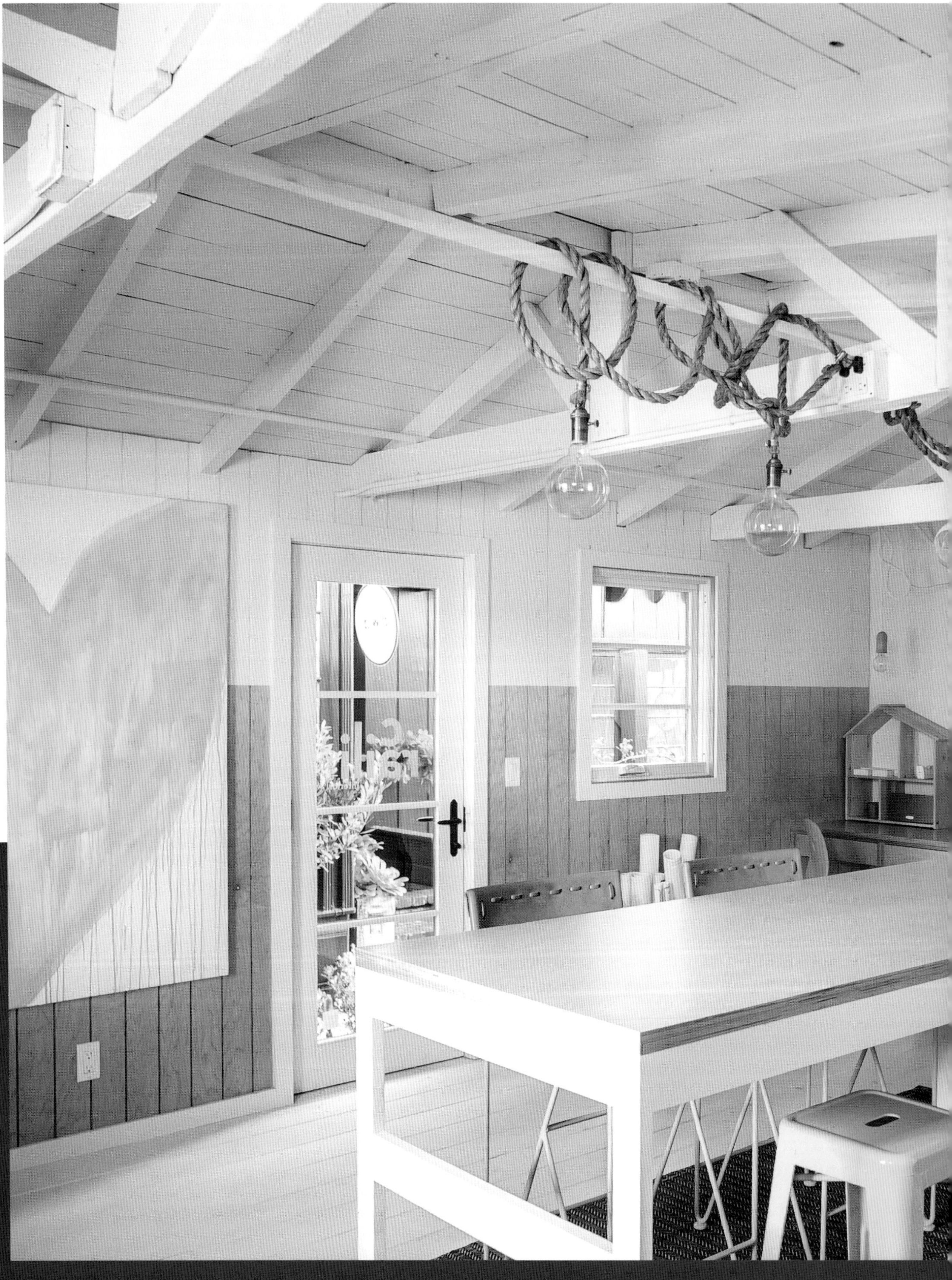

create a revolving mood board

Before I was an interior designer, my family had this plain-Jane drywall fireplace in our home. Every six months I had a blast doing something totally different and experimental with it.
I painted, wallpapered, decaled, and lettered that thing to my heart's content. Pick a spot in your home and let it be your safe place to go wild with your color experiments and see what sticks.
It's not going to kill you to paint your dad's violin (which, by the way, you're already planning to give to Goodwill) and put it up on the wall to see how it looks. It doesn't have to be permanent!

there's no wrong way to pop

Adding a pop of color into your home can feel like a chicken-or-the-egg sort of conundrum. But there's no right or wrong way to do this. If you're gaga over a box of pink tiles but aren't even sure what you're going to do with them, buy them! Your design will unfold after you set that pink tone for the room.

On the other hand, sometimes you'll look at a room you consider to be almost "done" and realize it needs a little somethin' somethin'. Adding a bright-blue chair to that space might be exactly what it is missing. You can have one little element in the room that's unexpected and flirty.

So, don't overthink it. The whole idea is to bring personality and cheerfulness into your house. Don't take yourself so seriously. Have *fun*.

GO WILD

Give a salty dog a new life—buy an old oil painting and dip it in yellow paint or make it talk. Cover your wall in blue polka dots or stripes. Powder-coat your lights, hooks, clothing hangers, or stools pink.

Add a big ole dose of sunshine with a can of yellow paint to arched doorways, transitions, and cabinet fronts.

Raili's Rainbow of Colors

When choosing a color to wake up your space, these are on my greatest-hits list:

Hot pink

Mustard

Dark navy blue

Olive green

Clary sage

Blue jean

Look in Your Closet

Let your threads be your guide! If you're trying to pinpoint what pop color speaks to you, look at your wardrobe. Chances are that a color that makes you feel good to wear will make you feel good every time you walk by it in your home.

Keep It Campy

When I was growing up, it wasn't in the family budget to send us kids away to sleepaway camp, but I always dreamed of going. All these years later, I'm living vicariously through my design clients when I add a campy feel to their kids' rooms, lounge rooms, playrooms, and the like. Camp is a place where people create special memories that stick with them forever. When Ryan and I sent our kids to surf camp, I only imagined all the fun they'd have surfing, kayaking, and even occasionally practicing archery. From my early imaginings of camp with brightly painted canoes to the surfboards lined up in all different colors at my kids' surf camp, it all looked like one giant art installation—even down to the screened-in bunk rooms. I want to bottle those memories and put them into homes through spaces that are whimsical, quirky, and totally campy.

This shot of vintage San Onofre brings back all my beach memories of crowded parking lots, dinged-up surfboards, and sunburned noses. Not to mention, all the cute boys.

pick your camp

Surf camp, lake camp, tennis camp, skate camp, band camp—pick your destination and lean into it! If you miss your sleepaway-camp days in the mountains, line a wall with a wilderness mural to transport you. Add wood paneling or shiplap to bring in those cabin vibes. Take it a step further and bring on the cabin by painting a paneled wall halfway up all the way around the room, including the door.

If your heart's still stuck at skate camp or tennis camp, decorate a wall with skateboards or old tennis rackets as an ode to your memories. For lake-camp vibes, track down some vintage fishing poles or water skis and prop 'em up or hang them on a wall. For surf camp, hang some fins on the wall.

out with the new, in with the old

With a camp theme, nothing should be too high-end or precious. This is a time when vintage reigns supreme, so keep your eye out for worn accessories or mementoes. For window treatments, try hanging up canvas instead of traditional curtains. Lay a vintage Pendleton blanket on the bed or couch. Use old-school lockers for storage instead of a cabinet or dresser.

I like to scour online marketplaces like Etsy and eBay to track down old and loved items that will whisk me off to nostalgia town. If you're on the hunt for particular pieces—retro first aid kits, maps, or other camp paraphernalia— let it be known among your family and friends. Let's just say my vintage thermos collection went from one to burgeoning after I alerted the masses that I was looking for some. This might be a cautionary tale, too; don't tell *everyone* you're looking for vintage compasses—maybe just a handful of people—or you might end up with a hundred of them.

I GOT TOP BUNK!

What would camp be without bunks? Every time I have a design project that involves bunk beds, I envision kids fighting over which bunk they want, and throwing pillows at all their snoring bunkmates.

bring on the kumbaya

Going to camp, whether it is sleepaway camp or camping somewhere with family and friends on the beach or in the mountains, stirs up a sense of community and casual sharing. I envision friends sitting around a mess hall swapping tall tales or a family gathered around a bonfire talking about their day. To recreate the playfulness and casualness of camp, keep it unstuffy. Inside, bring on the big floor cushions to encourage an air of fun and gathering. Outside, take it a step further and gather a bunch of chairs around a firepit. If you really want to keep the camp vibes alive, put a trailer in your backyard. I'm serious. Refurbish a Shasta or Airstream trailer to serve as your guest room, and it will be the instant trip to surf camp or mountain camp you never knew you needed.

Fly Your Fun Flag

Flags can scream "Camp!" at the drop of a hat. Whether you go for a pennant or a flag of the rectangle variety, shop on Etsy, eBay, or at flea markets for flags that echo your camp theme.

For surf camp, maybe you find a Slightly Choppy pennant that calls out your surf spot, like the Wedge. For lake camp, something with a canoe paddle on it could be awesome. You get the picture. Bonus points for flags that are older or vintage. Find a flag you connect with and put it up in your space. Here's a tip: hang a flag on a door (or perhaps the door that leads to your kids' room).

Raili's Camp-Vibes Checklist

When in doubt, add in these elements and you will almost hear the morning bugle wake-up call.

Something old or vintage that ties back to your favorite camp, like first aid kits or dart boards

Pendleton blankets or stripe motif

A retro collection of like items, such as thermoses or lanterns

A flag or two, the older the better

Industrial lighting

Found objects like shells, stones, or driftwood

Something red

Swiss-cross everything

Take a color or tone and run with it. If you're smitten with a denim-blue paint, pull in lighter and darker blues through rugs, pillows, and art. The tone-on-tone look lends well to ultra campy coziness.

It seems like everyone sticks to black and white when it comes to painting trim. To pull off a camp vibe, try a forest green paint for trim and doors. Pair that color with wood paneling, and you'll be singing campfire songs all the way to the lake.

For this kids' bunk-room locker wall, I used metal house numbers instead of traditional cabinet pulls. Everybody, remember your cubby number!

What's Your Type?

If there's a common theme I saw repeated in my twenty years working in the surf industry, it's that cool type—or words, rather—appears *everywhere*. I'm talkin' about sayings printed on T-shirts, surf-contest posters, and even beach signs. Over the years, these phrases or words stood out to me everywhere I went. Whether I saw a hand-painted "private beach" sign on a wall while headed down to the water to watch my husband surf or I spied a surf catchphrase on a Roxy or Quiksilver tee, these fun examples of type quickly stole my attention. I've always been inspired by how type interfaces with style and interacts with different environments. You just can't go wrong with a good saying.

In this kids' hangout space, we commissioned Jin-Woo Prensana for an extra-extra-large print of his famous "Venice" shot. It's a not-so-subtle reminder to be NICE.

what is it about words?

Whenever I work with a new client, nine times out of ten the first thing they say is, "We can't wait to see what words you want to use for the house." Using words or some sort of typeface in my designs is something I do in just about every home project I take on. You could say it's my thing. I must admit, I love using words, phrases, movie lines, song lyrics, and book excerpts anywhere I can. I have a hard time self-regulating, but my clients usually do that for me. No really, it's true. But I promise, there's a method to the mayhem.

Words and type bring personality, whimsy, and color into a space. A cheeky saying on your wall can be an icebreaker to visitors, but it's really a friendly beacon. I want my house (and your house) to be friendly. If I'm walking into a home and see a big sign on the wall that says "Can I kick it? Yes you can," I already know I'm going to like the people who live there and I'm going to have a good time. Incorporating type into your home will set a joyful tone and display your personality right off the bat.

cat got your tongue?

So, you're ready to use type in your home but you don't know what you want it to say. Start with your favorite song; pull out a lyric and put it on display: "Celebrate good times, c'mon." The same goes for favorite movie lines. "I've got chills, they're multiplying" would be a fitting saying to put near your wine fridge. Does your family have a go-to saying? Do you need a reminder to count your blessings? Put your tally up for all to see.

You can always count on surf lingo. The surf world is loaded with fun and quirky sayings. My husband, Ryan, will often say the waves are "two feet and firing," meaning they aren't big waves but they're still going to be fun. You also can't go wrong with an obvious description, like "bros" in a boys' bathroom or "groms" in a kids' bedroom.

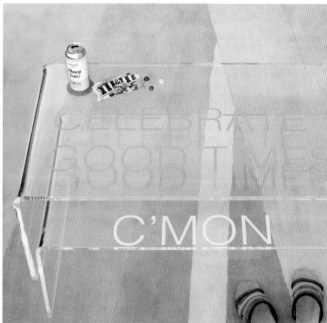

Once we hung the old-fashioned wallpaper in our home bar area, my friend came over and said, "This room doesn't feel like your style without some huge typography." And you know what? She was right. Aloha Amigo!

Pool houses have all the fun.
Take your favorite song lyric and
supersize it in pink neon lights.
Perfect Instagram moment.

you had me at hullo

I love to use words in different rooms throughout the house, but they make the most impact in the entryway. This is a great place to showcase your fun and effervescent personality from the get-go. Placing a phrase or saying at your entryway or front door also lifts your spirits as you come and go throughout your busy day. Maybe you need a friendly "Aloha Amigo" to greet you as you trudge through the front door after that long workday. Perhaps painting "hallo" on your front-porch decking or hanging an artwork with "Thanks and come again" on your entryway wall is what your home needs. Wherever you choose to say something, make it memorable and have fun with it.

AND A
THE
TREE
WAS
HAPPY A

Lighten Up

I had a client who wanted the phrase "Do good things in the world" displayed in the entryway of her home. I told her if I were a visitor, I'd probably think to myself, "That's a little serious; maybe I'm here for a laugh and a cocktail." Ask yourself, "Do I want my family, friends, and visitors to smile or feel challenged?"

OUTSIDE THE BOX

Type can be brought into design in obvious ways, such as art or signage, but thinking outside the box never fails to add extra oomph. Creative ways to use type include imprinting words into concrete sinks, carving words into wood surfaces like front doors or decking, or hanging pennants and flags. Heck, you can even have fun with your mailbox—they never get enough attention.

What's Your Type? 89

Name Your House

After taking many surf trips down to Baja, Mexico, I noticed that families commonly name their homes in Mexico (and in Hawaii, too). Our home in Baja is named La Caja, which translates to "box" . . . as in cash box; as in it's a black hole of cash we keep sinking money into. Name your home and flaunt it out front on a cool sign or at your front door.

Outside In

In surf culture there's an unmistakable connection between surfers and nature. Ask any waterman and they'll probably tell you about the serene, Zen-like feeling they get when they've paddled out and are sitting on their board, waiting for the next set to come in. Floating out in the ocean gives a whole new perspective of the trees and mountains on shore. It's a quiet unlike any other. Nature's pretty awesome like that, which is why I like to bring in the outdoors with every project I get my hands on. If you can't be close to the beach, being outside and enjoying the breeze and the sunshine on your face is the next best thing. Let's talk about making your outdoor space just as comfy as your indoor space—and we won't stop there. Indoor plants, full-blown plant installations, and trees that have a mind of their own are the best ways to bring that organic feeling inside.

The secret is creating a big ole vibe in the front yard and backyard and carrying that all the way through the house.

landscape your living spaces

Sure, indoor plants are cool and all, but have you ever put a full-on tree in your house? Lined your entire hallway with potted figs on both sides? No? Well, why not? I love to reimagine how plants are used inside the home and push beyond the boundaries of a traditional plant in a pot that's stuck in the corner of the room.

If I could have a real-life indoor tree (planted in the ground) in every home I design, I would. But that's not always the easiest to pull off, so the next best option is what I like to call "fully invasive indoor trees." Don't pick out a plant that perfectly fits in the corner of the room. Instead, bring home the tree whose branches are going east and west and everywhere in between. The more the tree spreads out and starts running into things, the better. These beautiful, sloppy trees create a continuation from the front yard all the way throughout the home and back outside again.

Raili's Favorite Indoor Plants

Ficus Audrey

Snake plant

Candelabra cactus

Philodendron "Lickety Split"

Opuntia cactus

Aralia Fabian

Beyond wild trees, there are so many outside-the-box ways to use plants inside the home. Think of it as creating a mini jungle in a part of the home that feels boring or devoid of life. A long blank wall or a bench near a window might be the best place to add a built-in plant installation.

mi patio es tu patio

If you're not making your outdoor space feel as comfortable as the inside to maximize your home's full potential, you don't know what you're missing. Take your favorite rooms in the house and translate that style to the yard or patio. A dining or bar and seating area will beckon you to bring your dinner or glass of wine and book outside and remember just how amazing it feels to connect with nature. Rugs, side tables, fun light fixtures, and cozy furniture you want to collapse into all make the inside of a house feel special, and the same goes for your deck and yard. Hang art outside! Giving the same thoughtful detail to the outdoor space as you do to the inside of your home will guarantee you, your family, and guests will always have a memorable spot to veg out and make some memories.

Now, before you get all "business in the front, party in the back" when you start scheming the décor for your outdoor digs, remember this: if you have an outdoor space of any kind, whether it's a big yard or a small patio, the goal is to echo the design inside to the outside. I hate to break it to ya, but it's not going to feel right to have it be scando inside and Taj Mahal on the outside-trust me. If you're committed to bringing surf style to your home, you need to ride that wave from the moment it starts to crest through to the end.

come in, the water's fine

If you can't have the Pacific at your front door, adding a water element of some sort will still give you those coastal feels. Water, whether you're looking at it or listening to it, brings out that relaxing element.

At one design project, we brought in an old vessel from a stone yard and created an unconventional fountain with a spigot that was installed above the vessel. The vessel contains a recirculating water pump, so water continuously flows through the spigot and into the stone vessel below. It was a small but impactful feature that brings the same tranquility you'd experience if there was a creek or bubbling stream nearby.

Birdbaths are probably the most low-maintenance water features you can choose and a great first step to experimenting with water elements at home.

To take it a step further, a cedar hot tub feels very much like surf camp and checks off the water box. My favorite thing about a body of water larger than a fountain or birdbath is the way the sky and surrounding trees reflect off it.

Be it a baby birdbath or a pool, see where you can add a splash of water to your yard or patio and notice what a mood booster it can be. Sit back, close your eyes, and you'll almost feel the saltwater spray if you try hard enough.

home is where the yard is

The best way to ensure you have the *most* fun in your outdoor space is to first think about how you'll live in it. If you're a family with young kids and a pool, perhaps you need a seating area near the water so you can watch your kiddos swim. If you have teenagers, they probably need a place where they can kumbaya with their friends away from the house. Word to the wise: teens don't like formal dining tables, and they like to have their own space. In fact, mine gather around a firepit with their friends outside our reclaimed Shasta camper in the backyard.

Answer your needs but don't get too formal with it. Bring on the pillows and make the outdoors an interactive place where you can drag over a stool to join a conversation. If you're going to live in this space, really make it suitable for life.

Raili's Favorite Outdoor Materials

Natural decking

Teak

Grass

Gravel

Brick

DON'T FORGET THE SHOWER

My surfing kiddos will tell you that showering outside after a day of surfing is as good as it gets. If you have space in your backyard—maybe close to your pool or primary bathroom—adding an outdoor shower will give you that fresh-from-the-waves feeling at home.

pass-throughs for the win(dow)

If you have a kitchen window that faces out to your backyard, that is the perfect opportunity to have a pass-through window. Adding a bar top below that window from the outside will give that open feeling and take your outdoor entertaining up a notch. Whether it's where you pass margaritas to guests or burgers headed for the grill, or where the kids swing by to grab a popsicle, this touch never fails to put the fun in function.

Speaking of fun, uniting your inside and outdoor spaces doesn't need to stop with the pass-through. Café doors, wide sliding Dutch doors, or nano doors are the perfect connectors between inside and outside. Open 'em up and invite 'em all in.

GET LIT

A nighttime party outside is like nothing else, and it truly feels magical when the lighting is just right. Hang a cluster of light fixtures over a pod of chairs to create a reimagined ceiling. String up paper lanterns and twinkle lights. Gather groupings of hurricane lanterns or candles around your seating areas and you'll have ambiance for days.

WINDOWS = FRAMES

If you have a big window in your house with a cool vantage point, plant a cactus garden or a cluster of trees right outside. And if you really want to make it extra, add landscape lighting and voilà—au naturel art.

break on through to the other side

As you paddle out to connect your inside spaces to your outdoor ones, remember that it all starts at the front door and front yard. Your first impression of your home should set the tone for what's to come inside and back outside again. Start with big, beautiful trees in your front yard—as many as you can fit. Line your halls and rooms with indoor plants and keep that plant party going in the back. Keep your hallways green—literally. In one of my projects, we were planning to install a long built-in bench, but a window in the middle of the wall gave us the idea to put a planter in that bench (bottom middle).

TREES > BUSHES

Trees always win over bushes to frame the exterior of your house. Start with the tree and build a trellis around it. The branches will give you an instant outdoor ceiling.

6 Tile with a Smile

When I think of tile, my brain instantly goes back to long beach days as a kid. The public beach bathrooms had the best tile. I'm talking about those almost industrial tiled bathrooms where you might have seen "NO RUNNING" spelled out in red square tiles in a sea of white. Or at the pool where "NO DIVING" was tiled into the floor in the shallow end. There's something about those retro tile moments that I'm always trying to bring back. They remind me of old-school beach culture.

Tile is a great opportunity to add personality to areas that aren't as central to the home, like powder rooms, laundry rooms, bars, and pool houses. Whether you bust out the color, pattern, or words, use tile as a chance to let your hair down a bit.

tile outside the box

Putting tile on a wall is a great idea, but have you tried tiling behind built-in shelving or inside of a sink? Or up and over an enclosed shower wall like a totally awesome Aviator Nation–inspired retro border? Instead of tiling just behind the sink in your guest bathroom, take the tile from the floor and run it all the way up the wall for major impact. Better yet, make a tile "rug" or moment: have your contractor install your wood flooring with a tile inlay to designate special rooms or boundaries.

If you want to do something really unexpected and fun with tile, install it all the way around the threshold in a doorway, from floor to wall to ceiling and back down again. Bonus points for using blue handcrafted tiles that make you feel like you're walking through the curve of a big wave. One of my favorite tile moments involved a graphic black-and-white tile that we ran from the floor all the way up the backsplash behind the sink and to the ceiling. It was neat to see how the tile and the wood flooring met to make for a cool powder room.

Whatever color you go with, this tile treatment signifies the transition from room to room in a memorable way.

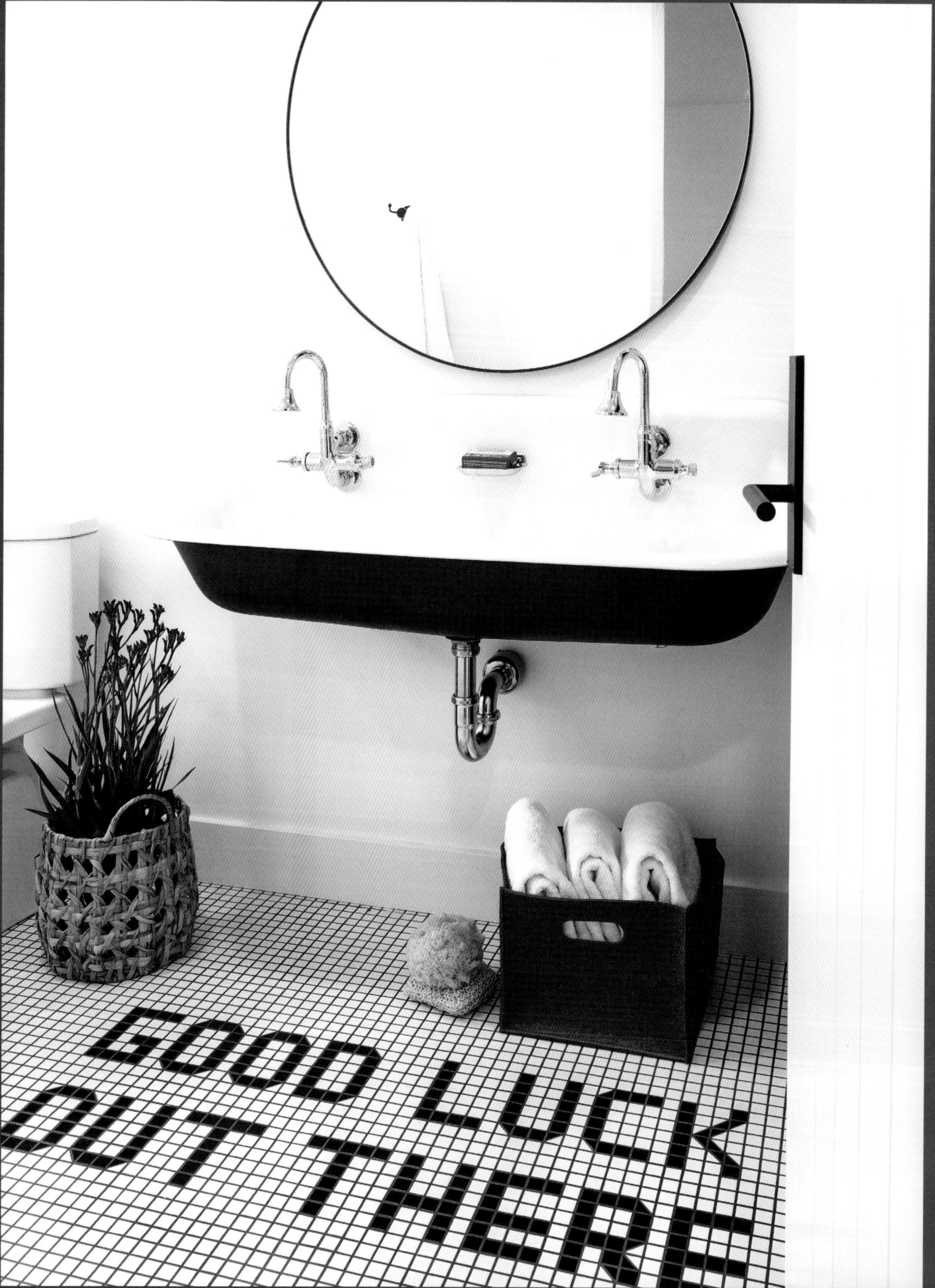
GOOD LUCK
OUT THERE

time for a tile tattoo

Looking back on my original tile inspo from my childhood, using tile to spell out words is so fantastic that once you try it, it's hard to stop. What can I say? This blends my love of typography and tile in all the right ways. The shape of tile naturally lends itself to creating a rad typeface because of its hard lines, so this is yet another way to infuse a space with personality or type. For a kids' bathroom, install your tile to say, "Good luck out there," or in your powder room, go with a cheeky "Oh hey."

And don't nix the niche—that's right, that inset part of your shower wall where you keep your shampoo and conditioner. That's an often-overlooked space that could instantly become epic if you tiled it with a word of your choice. I'd go with something surfy, like "Yo," to keep that shower funky and fresh. Every shower has a niche, but the standard formula is just tiling it with a piece of stone. But what about putting a saying or some hot-pink tile in there?

Warning: Installing words in tile is not for the faint of heart. Using tile to unleash your inner songwriter or comedian is like getting a tattoo. If you end up wanting to change it, it will be pricey and difficult to remove. Make sure you think long and hard about what message you want to send to yourself . . . and everyone else!

three cheers for cement tile

Morocco has nailed this look from the early days with their graphic printed tile. The time I got started in the design world coincided with the surge and new popularity of cement tile. Cement tiles have a timeless, handcrafted look to them because they're, well, handcrafted. That also gives them a boatload of personality compared to ceramic tiles that are manufactured to look identical. This worn-in look feels beachy and surfy to me. I love to use cement tiles to create Swiss cross motifs, pull off a checkerboard look (for a nod to Vans, of course), or bring in some pattern play. Moroccan cement tiles' use of color and pattern takes the playful level of boring stock tile from one to ten.

hue gotta use these colors

Tile is a great opportunity to bring some color into your space, and I have some go-to colors I reach for again and again because they are sure to bring a smile every time. If you want to feel connected to the ocean, go for blue tones. Yellow will bring in that ray of sunshine, and a super-hot pink will give your home a flavor all on its own. A white-and-black checkerboard look is both classic and just plain fun—you can't go wrong.

Using colored tile can help you bring in throwback vibes or be that *wow* moment in an otherwise neutral room. Try creating a half wall with tile or tile the whole wall but with two slightly varying shades of green—one on the top and one on the bottom. This will create a tonal feel that is super pretty and super coastal.

Not every bathroom is lucky enough to get a skylight. The natural light beaming on the zellige tile turns the shower walls into an art installation.

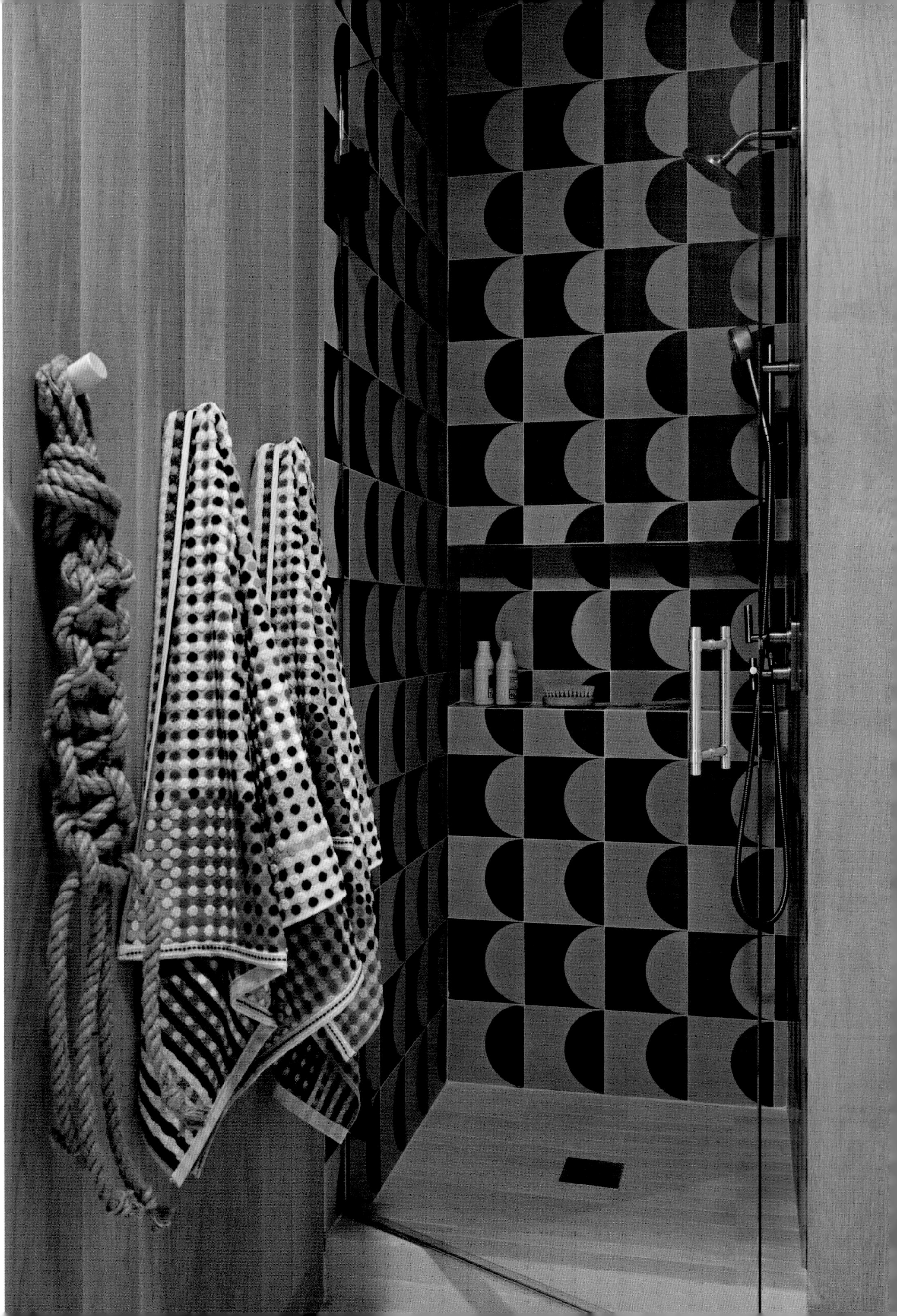

Concrete Collaborative (below, left) is a team favorite at Raili CA Design. I'm also a sucker for a handmade Moroccan tile (below, right) like this one from Mission Tile West.

Raili's Favorite Tile Brands

HEATH CERAMICS
Heath is a hand-firing operation in Sausalito, California, that started in 1948. What I love about Heath is the colors they use and that no two tiles are the same. When you put tiles in the same colorway up on a wall, it's like a piece of artwork because each tile has a different saturation of color. Their Verde, Turmeric, and Grove tiles are some of my favorites.

CONCRETE COLLABORATIVE
I may be partial to Concrete Collaborative because I have a collaboration with them, but they are without a doubt the king and queen of fun tile. I've done a hot-pink terrazzo tile with them before and a half-circle style that looks like a sun. They love to get a little wild without going overboard, and that's what I'm all about.

CLÉ
I love this brand because they have the best selections of Zellige tiles and beautiful exposed, unfinished glazed brick.

Stripe's Away

One way to bring that '70s surf vibe to your space is to add retro stripes of tile that cut through a wall or shower with a different color than most of the tiles installed in the same area. For example, maybe you have an all-white tiled shower, but you add in a blue stripe somewhere. Perhaps your stripes go through your shower niche or even carry across the wall behind your vanity.

If These Walls Could Talk

Surfboards are usually a reflection of the person who owns them. Whether it's fun stickers, a bold color, or stripes, adding some flair to your board distinguishes it from other surfers' boards, and I like to think of our home in the same way.

A clean white wall is just like a blank canvas or a surfboard blank. The first thing someone creative says when they look at a blank canvas is, "What am I going to put on that canvas?" While some people are into that neutral-everywhere-all-the-time look, I approach it by asking, "What's zippy and fun? What emotes a little bit of personality?"

I'm not into cookie-cutter replicas—let's mark our territory and set our home apart from everybody else's. Let's engrave our personality on our walls through hand-painted treatments, wallpaper, half walls, stripes, polka dots, photo murals, and more—just like the surfers do with their boards.

hand-painted and totally '80s

I love wallpaper—and we'll get to that in a minute—but there is something refreshingly custom and unique about hand-painted wall treatments. If I want a room to feel like my teen years, I'm going to deck it out with hand-painted polka dots or run a retro stripe up and over and around a bedroom wall. This is my way of channeling my pal Danny Kwock, a surf legend who helped cement the introduction of bold colors and patterns in the surf world when he started surfing Newport's Echo Beach in his neon Quiksilver shorts in the '80s. When Echo Beach exploded with color from these fresh new designs, surfers painted their boards with bright polka dots and vibrant colors to stand out and match their equally loud shorts.

These patterns and colors are still with me, and they do wonders in taking spaces from plain Jane to clever and lively. Go for a big polka-dot pattern all over one wall of your kid's room or bathroom. Put a big bull's-eye in your game room. Run a multicolor stripe from your teen's bathroom out and into the bedroom—heck, you can paint that bad boy over the bed, from drywall onto wood paneling, and make a serious splash.

the writing's on the wall

Speaking of hand-painted, sometimes in design you're faced with a big, blank twenty-foot wall and you have no idea what to do to fill it. Sure, you could leave it blank and move on with your life, or you could use it as an opportunity to say something interesting.

When I was faced with one such wall and was racking my brain over what to do with it, my husband introduced me to the work of Matthew Allen, an artist on Instagram. Matt had this cool print that said "Count Your Blessings" with lots of tally marks underneath the wording. In two seconds I messaged Matt and said, "Can you do this same thing but on a twenty-five-foot wall?" Thankfully he said yes! After two days, some scaffolding, black paint, and lots and *lots* of tally marks, the "Count Your Blessings" idea was now super-sized in my stairwell on that once-sad blank wall.

This call to action provides a clever moment when someone is walking down the stairs, and I've definitely never seen it in another house before.

be in the spot

Photos are awesome, but *big* photos are even better. A photo mural of your favorite place puts you right in the spot, literally. If you have a photo that's good quality, chances are it can be made into a mural that covers your wall and transports you to *vacaciones* in an instant.

A photo mural is a great addition to the bar, dining room, game room, kids' room, pool house, office, or hallway. Maybe you already know you want to put in a photo mural of the California coastline or a curling wave—go for it! If you don't know where to start with picking your photo, think of what your family likes to do for fun or where you like to travel. If you don't want to use one of your photos, browse shots from your favorite photographer or peruse free-download websites and type in search terms like "skateboard girls," "waves," or "balloons"—whatever makes you happy. Incorporating the history of your home or location is also a good way to go, so check out historical archives in your city. If you find an image you'd like to use, ask if you can have the rights to print the photo as a mural.

Lastly . . . I almost always print photo murals in black and white. Printing a large color photo for the wall will dictate the color of the room's design and pigeonhole you into sticking with that same color palette. If you like to shake things up with your furniture pieces, keep the photo mural black and white.

There are companies that will print your photo to mural size; just make sure the photo you've selected is high resolution. Oh, and have fun! These photo murals are great ways to insert meaningful family moments and personality into the home.

wild about wallpaper

The great thing about wallpaper is that it's graphic and colorful—at least *my* favorite patterns and designs are. It can be that one last thing to add to a space that just *makes* the whole room. If you want to stay neutral with your furniture and not take big color risks, adding a bold wallpaper is the perfect compromise. Since so many wallpapers are made to be peel and stick, you can really lean into a fun pattern knowing it can come down when and if you get sick of it.

And I'm not just talking about wallpapering regular ole walls. Wallpaper can be used in small doses and in unexpected places: behind a bar or built-in bookshelf or on the ceiling of a powder room, for starters. You can even wallpaper an interior door in your home to give it a wink. Adding just a sliver of wallpaper to a room can take it from snore to score, I promise. If you really want to go for it, hand-letter over that paper. What a kick!

half walls

I'm obsessed with half walls. What's a half wall, you say? It's where you paint half a wall one color and the other half a totally different color. I love using half walls in my designs because they make me think of the ocean and the horizon beyond.

Whether one half is blue and the other half white, or olive green and black, or slightly different tones from one half to the other, this paint trick adds a lot of pizazz and architectural interest to a room. You can even apply this treatment to paneled walls, so you have full permission to half wall to your heart's content.

SUPERSIZE MY ARTWORK, PLEASE

This is kinda the same idea as the photo mural but in a different application. If you have a spot in your house with a lot of wall space, that's an excuse to use supersized artwork: one large piece of art on one large wall. From your bathroom to your office, don't be afraid to play with scale and fill the whole wall with a framed artwork that sets the tone for the room. Photos of kids' faces at five feet high by five feet wide are more fun than normal size.

GALLERY WALLS,
RAILI STYLE

I know, I know: You've heard of a gallery wall before. All the cool kids are doing it. I get it. But when I put up a gallery of artwork onto a wall, I like to mix in some unexpected items. Add in different textures and colors with your frames—a red flag, a little hat, maybe some surf fins. Incorporating these different elements will really help tell your story and let the wall do the talking.

8
It's All in the Details

Picture this: You find yourself with a room that feels pretty done and dusted. The furniture is awesome, you laid down a cool rug, you have a plant that doesn't mind its p's and q's, but the room still feels a little flat. When I design a space, this is the moment when I walk in and I don't know what's going to happen next. All I know is we need to spice it up with some details. This is when the real fun begins!

WILD HORSES OF SABLE ISLAND
Roberto Dutesco

Henri Matisse

Y OF **BASEBALL** BOWMAN/ZOSS

JAMES TAYLOR

Don't sleep on art and accessories—they simply *make* the room. If you've got your space mostly figured out with the big stuff, look around and see what else it needs. Maybe you bring in a chair and dip the legs in brightly colored paint. Perhaps you wrap your ceiling beams with rope or add a checkerboard-patterned pillow to your couch. Maybe that huge light fixture brings the drama you were so badly missing. Add in natural elements you find in nature (jute, rattan, wicker, or natural wood) and art that reminds you of your best summer vacation ever to bring that surf style through. It's these details that make all the other things in the room sing.

There isn't a rhyme or reason to adding these textures and details to a room. It sometimes comes as a game-time decision. Like deciding to catch a wave. Look at your space and see what it needs. If you have a lot of black, do you need to warm it up with some leather? Do you have a large area that needs something equally large in scale? Do you have any rope? Should you nail a rug to the floor like your favorite Ralph Lauren store? Play around and have fun adding in the details that let your surf-culture vibes come alive.

rope is dope

I have a lifelong fascination with wrapping things in rope, starting with the handlebars of my bike when I was a kid. Aside from wrapping rope around anything I could find, I also tried my hand at some basic rope wall-hanging. My mom was a macramé whiz and taught me one basic knot, and I made everything I could think of with that knot. I made wall hangings and things to hang on the doorknob of my room. I was in deep with rope at a young age.

SHOW ME THE ROPES

I can't mention rope without shouting out my friend, Laguna Beach macramé artist Jim Olarte. A self-described beachcomber, Jim uses driftwood he finds washed up onshore and new sailing rope to weave jaw-dropping macramé pieces. Many of my projects, including Kelly Slater's Surf Ranch, were taken to the next level when I hung up his rope wonders on display.

Now I can't look at a surface or object without thinking, "Can I wrap that in rope?"

It makes sense that rope has stuck with me all this time, from my beach days as a kid to my design projects as an adult: rope gives that nod to maritime culture, beach culture, and nautical style. It takes something ordinary and gives it texture and personality.

Take, for instance, plumbing fixtures for your sink. If you have a sink with exposed plumbing fixtures in your powder room, wrap them in rope. Take your ho-hum stair rails and twist that rope around the spindles. Give your ceiling beams the rope makeover and see an instant difference. Reimagine your table legs and light fixtures. If you want to take it to the next level, wrap your surfboard with rope and put it on display as a knockout art installation. Swap in rope for the nylon cords on your light fixtures. Amazon and other retailers sell rope that's wired for electrical, so you can go to town with a naughty knotty rope light installation.

My favorite ropes to use are cotton and jute. Cotton rope reminds me of California beach culture, and jute feels a little more mountainy and rustic. You can't go wrong with either. Look around your space and see where you can add some rope to bring home that beach feeling.

Raili's Favorite Places to Use Rope

Light fixtures

Plumbing fixtures

Beams

Stair rails

Hardware

Chair legs

Table legs

When it comes to wrapping things with rope, the method slightly varies based on what you're attaching it to. On plastic—such as an unsightly plastic plumbing piece I want to disguise—I first tie the knot behind the plumbing and then start wrapping the rope around tightly. Once I've covered the whole surface with wrapped rope, I tie the ends tightly in the back to secure the rope; the same goes for beams. On metal hardware or pulls, I glue the end of the rope onto the surface with a glue gun and start wrapping around tightly to cover.

Rope It Yourself

You can make rope hardware and accessories yourself with a little bit of creativity. To go even deeper down the rabbit hole of rope, here are a few features you can make around the house with rope:

For a standard door or barn door, tie a rope knot in place of the doorknob. The same goes for cabinet doors or handles or dresser drawers.

Take a glue gun and affix a continuous length of rope around the outside edges of a mirror.

Grab some T-bars from your local hardware store, hot-glue them with a bit of rope, and hang them on a wall for a neat hook for hats, bags, and swim fins.

Make a unique toilet paper holder out of a knotted loop of rope that's attached to the wall.

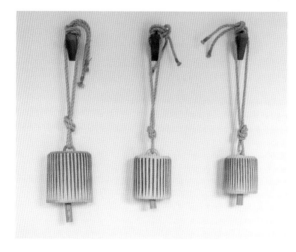

surfing cowboy

Step aside, other textures: leather is here, and it might as well be the Gerry Lopez (one of my favorite surfers) of the design world—the terribly handsome, quiet, cool guy at a party. Just like rope, one of my favorite materials to accessorize with is leather. Leather adds a dash of rustic to a space, which can blend so well with beach or nautical style (think California cowboy meets California surfer). It's also the cool factor you might be missing from your space. It's the swagger. It's a layer of texture. And most importantly, it adds color without being a color.

For example, if you prefer a more neutral space, leather can take it from feeling sterile and one-note to warm and welcoming. Whether it's through a larger piece, such as a chair or an ottoman, or something smaller, such as leather-lined hardware or a leather décor accessory on your coffee table, even the smallest amount takes a room to a new level of sophistication.

The best part about leather is the way it wears. For Kelly Slater's Surf Ranch (below), we incorporated a good dose of leather because we knew the pieces would get lots of love in such a high-traffic spot while delivering that hip element. Once leather has been sat on, skimmed past, and beat up a bit, it comes to life.

Bonus points: Pair your leather with wood. Trust me on this. Think of leather-front cabinets inset into wood. It's a natural look that's elevated without saying, "Hey, look at me." Leather cabinet pulls will also bring in that same feel for an easier update on a wooden dresser or wood cabinet doors.

WRAP IT IN LEATHER

You can use leather twine in the same ways as rope on cabinet hardware, beams, stair rails, and more.

check yourself

When I think of surf, I think of skateboards; and when I think of skateboards, I think of checkerboard print. And I can't talk about checkerboard print without mentioning Vans. My husband, Ryan, spent sixteen years working for Vans, a California–based skateboarding shoe company that is the epicenter of checkerboard shoes and a big part of '80s surf culture. If I were to utter the word *rad*, it would be in reference to checkerboard pattern. Checkerboard is in my DNA.

While Vans brought checkerboard predominantly to the skateboarding fashion scene, Quiksilver took that black-and-white baton and carried it forward with spirit. Checkerboard pattern is timeless, but it's also a *moment* in time for me: when I see checkerboard, I immediately think of Vans, surf culture, and what everyone was wearing at the beach back when I used to take the bus down to Seal Beach.

This is a print that can look laid-back or elegant, depending on how it's applied. Try it out on wallpaper, pillows, artwork, tile, rugs, and anywhere else your checkered brain will take you.

Tiles in black-and-white marble will send the iconic pattern into a whole new kingdom of sophistication. Hang some skateboards on a checkerboard-wallpapered wall and make your kid's bedroom into a mellow chill zone.

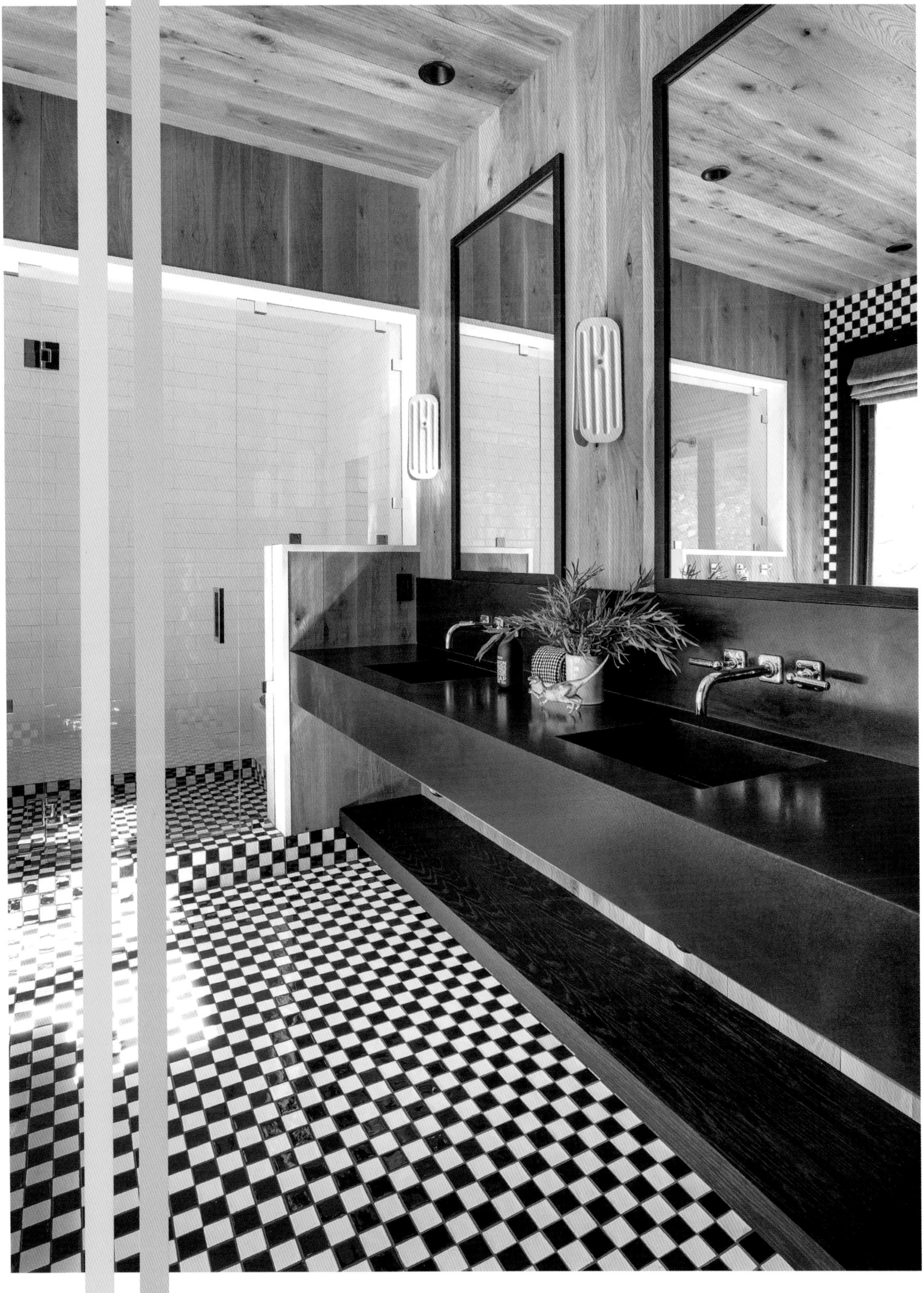

messy-beds club

I have a confession: I do not know how to properly make a formal bed with tight hospital corners. I hope we can still be friends. And you know what? I don't know how to make a formal bed like that by choice. Here's why: When I see a bed that's messy and unmade, it looks more inviting to me. It says, "Get on in here with your fuzzy socks and your book and stay awhile!" To me, a formal bed feels like more of a chore to turn down and hop into.

A messy bed can change the feeling of a bedroom; it makes it feel more casual and inviting. I'm not talking about a bed that's totally blown up—it's organized mess we're seeking. To pull off this look, double up on your comforters so you have a mountain of blankets, scrunch down your top sheets so they resemble a wave, and stagger your pillows so they aren't in perfect rows. If you're hyper-ventilating over this and don't have it in you to go full mess, let's compromise. Throw a blanket over the end of your bed—don't fold it perfectly; let it relax. Let your hair down a little.

go big or go home

One detail that can really spice up your space is *scale*—big scale. There are three things I like to supersize when it comes to scale: light fixtures, artwork, and plants. Take what you would normally go for with size and dial that baby up a few notches. Hang some gigantic pendant lights over your dining table (but be mindful of sightline when sitting and looking at your dinner mate). Blow up your favorite photo and let it shout. Kick out your little plant in the corner and replace it with a nine-foot tree.

Black and White and Wood All Over

If you're into surf style but you're not a fan of all those wild colors, I get it. How about a compromise? Let's keep the vibe but tone it down by using black, white, and wood. Vintage longboards and old-school woodies were staples in surf culture back in the day and serve as great inspiration for interiors. And a classic black-and-white surf-film poster, like Don Brown's 1961 *Surf's Up*, never goes out of style.

Using black, white, and wood as a base is a one-size-fits-all design palette that can be used in any room of the house. Pairing black and white makes a strong statement, and the wood softens the whole look and keeps it au naturel. All you need to do after that is BYOF: Bring Your Own Fun.

paint it black

Black is moody, dramatic, and downright cool. Black is the leather jacket of the room. It says, "I'm going to catch your eye but I'm not being desperate about it because I'm effortlessly fantastic." Whether you bring in black through accents—this would be sticking your pinky toe in the pool—or paint your kitchen cabinets black, this color makes a bold but casual statement.

For black paint options, including paint-grade cabinets, my go-to colors are Benjamin Moore "Wrought Iron" and Farrow and Ball "Railings." Both hues are technically a very deep charcoal, which is key to bringing in a dose of black that still feels warm and inviting. For a stain-grade surface like trim or cabinets, a good ole black stain looks even better than paint because it lets the wood grain come through.

Black can also be used in the form of stone. A dark leathered granite, dark limestone, or dark soapstone can be your nonpaint pop of black (think bathroom and kitchen countertops or fireplace surrounds).

white lightning

Okay, "lightning" might be a bit of a stretch because the white in this design palette is meant to temper the black harmoniously. It's there to serve as a backbone of the room and not do all the talking. In essence, white is the classic white T-shirt of the room. You gotta have something to layer the leather jacket over, right?

In my black, white, and wood combo, white is usually used in the form of paint. And I'm not talking about the stark white paint you see on the walls at a gallery. When you marry white with black, your white needs to have some warmth and soul to it for the whole thing to work. Benjamin Moore "Chantilly Lace" and Sherwin-Williams "Pure White" are my favorites because they're crisp without all the blue undertones.

Your something-white in a space can, of course, be drywall, but if I had my druthers, I would add white shiplap instead of plain drywall. White always looks better when it is applied to an architectural detail.

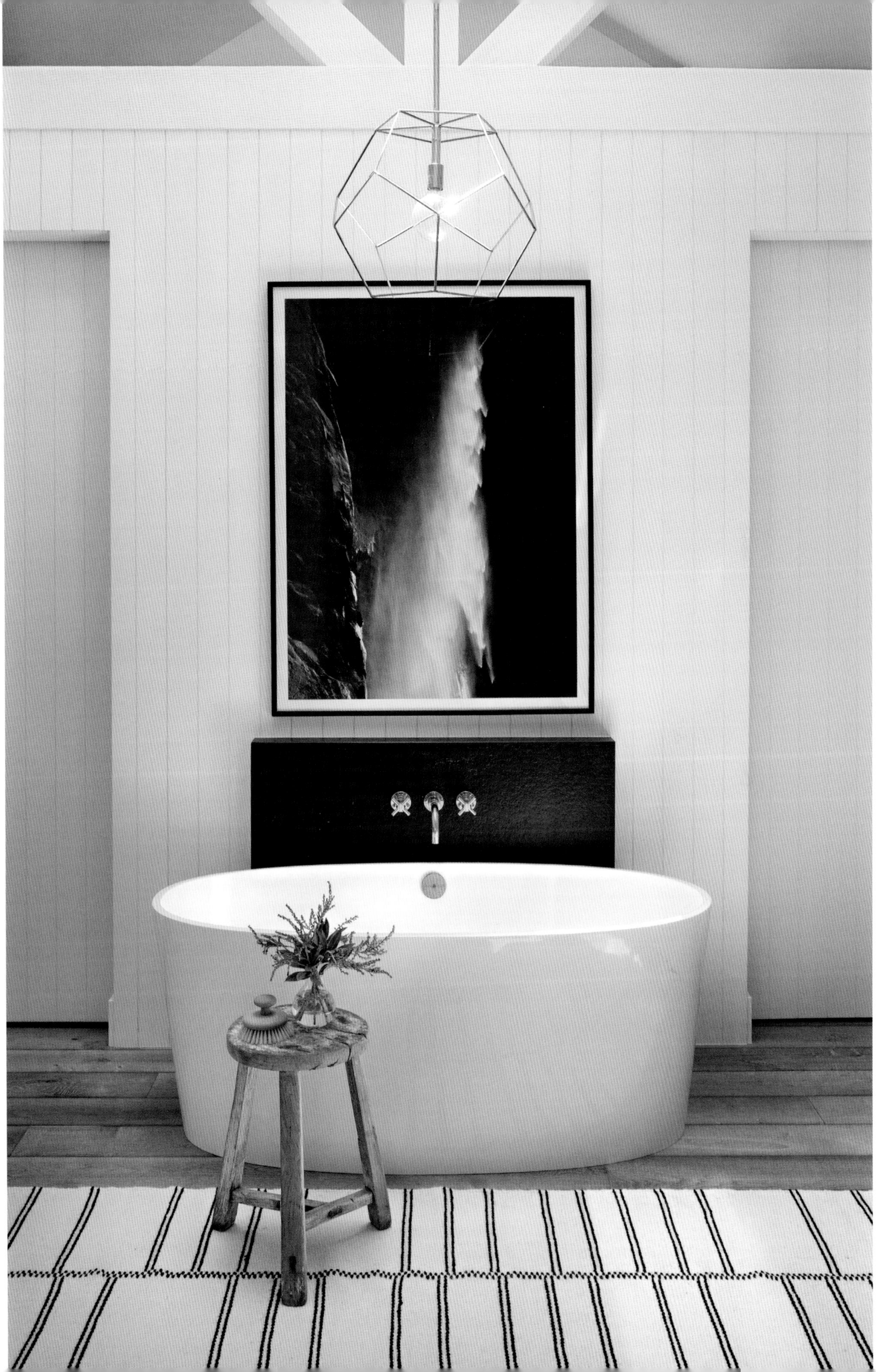

I am never afraid of mixing wood species. In fact, there are four different species of wood in this great room: rift oak, Douglas fir, cedar, and plain sawn oak. They all play nicely together.

wood is a color

Black and white is a powerful pair, but you don't want everything to look like an Oreo cookie. That's where the wood comes in. Wood is our classic pair of jeans—stick with me on this outfit analogy; it ties together the white T and the black leather jacket in a timeless, easy-going, and memorable way.

When pairing with black and white, wood that is not painted but left with its original color works best. Wood can be used in a tongue-and-groove ceiling feature, as hardwood flooring, as exposed beams in the ceiling, in wall paneling, on an epic bedframe or headboard, on a fireplace mantle, on a kitchen island, through chairs and accessories, and so much more. Just keep in mind that your wood element needs a friend to bring it all together. If you choose to use hardwood floors, bring in wood elsewhere on the ceiling, in decorative pieces, and so on.

When deciding on how to add wood to a room, it's like choosing a paint color and is super important in designing a room. For example, a rift sawn white oak reads sophisticated, whereas a plain sawn oak has a little bit more of a wild personality. Once you select your wood, your style can start evolving in the home.

I've always been addicted to boardwalks at the beach and that translates to all the projects where I use wood siding. When it comes to interiors, don't shy away from natural wood because it's going to bring in the California cool.

Raili's Favorite Types of Wood

1 PINE
for a style that leans more Scandinavian

2 WHITE OAK
for a more sophisticated look

3 WALNUT
for a rich, modern vibe

4 MAHOGANY
for a little taste of Hawaii

5 CEDAR
for more of a surf, mountain, or outdoorsy feel

BRING ON THE PLANTS

If you want to bring a dash of color and interest into this more neutral palette, bring in plants. A green plant in front of a black backdrop never fails to make me giddy. Come to think of it, same with art—everyone thinks of hanging art on a white wall but the right pieces can pop perfectly off a black painted wall.

CHECK ALL YOUR BOXES

Bring in more layers through leather accessories to add a noncolor color. Bring in some rope (page 160) to build warmth through textures. And if hardwood floors just aren't your thing, go for a black-and-white-checkered floor (hello, Vans) to keep things refreshing within your controlled color palette.

The perfect blend of black, white, and wood—but on a BIG scale. For this entertainer's pad, we ran white oak paneling vertically up the wall to play with the stellar ceiling height.

We're Not in Newport Anymore

You don't have to be west of the I-5 to get that surf-style feel in your home and all the energizing, casual uniqueness that comes with it. You can completely reimagine surf culture in any home, whether you're in the mountains, the country, the city, and beyond. Surf style is ultimately about releasing your inner fun and taking a chance. Just because you don't have waves at your front door doesn't mean you can't capture that mood wherever you live. As you'll see in this final chapter, blending all the ideas together from this book and leaning into it will result in a home that is fearless, fabulous, and fun.

10

vacation mode activated

My design clients in states outside of California want to bring home surf style because they feel a connection to surfing or the beach in some way. Maybe they take a trip to the coast every summer and want to pay tribute to their memories. Or maybe when they visit the beach, they leave their laptop behind and become a totally different person. An emotional attachment to the beach has imprinted on them and they can't shake it in the best way.

I get it. It's kinda like whenever I travel and visit a cool boutique hotel or new-to-me restaurant or shop. I always come away from my trip more inspired because some of these hotels and places take design chances that stick with me. These are often things the average person wouldn't try at home because it feels a bit too outside-the-box. But why should we stop with that visionary experimentation when it comes to the place where we spend the most time? Surfers and my favorite watermen and beachcombers are some of the most creative people I know. Our homes should be rotating galleries of weird, of "Well, let's give this a try," and things that make us giggle or spark a sweet memory.

This is me giving you full permission to turn that knob to funky and loosen up. Take your favorite vacation moments and memories and bring them to life. Having glimpses of these punchy, welcoming details in your lake home, your mountain home, or landlocked elsewhere will always bring you back to the beach and that spirit of surf.

With views like these, all-natural materials were a must for this great room. Unfinished leathers, rustic woods, and textural rugs elevate the space without stealing the show.

fake it till you make it

There is so much more to surf style than sticking a surfboard in a room . . . but that certainly helps play up the "surf" part of the whole shebang. Hang a surfboard on a wall horizontally above a bed, prop it up in a corner, wrap it in rope and hang it vertically in your bathroom. One of the best bets for feelin' surfy is, well, to add surf stuff. Same goes for fins. Hang a collection of swim fins on the wall and it will feel like an art installation.

Since surf and skate cultures are endlessly intertwined—they're like PB&J—hang some skateboards on a checkerboard wallpaper to bring out that West Coast attitude.

Elements that are rooted in surf and beach culture—rope, surfboards, fins, and skateboards—can take you to the sand (mentally) without feeling too theme-y. The key is to balance these features within a room so they're little moments that remind you of your favorite place without feeling like a surf shop.

reinvent
the board

From a sport that saw early surfers surfing on redwood boards to the fiberglass/polyurethane/epoxy combo we see today, reinvention is old hat in the surf world. It keeps things interesting. That's how I like to look at design: I look around a room and say, "How can I make this more fun? How can I turn this on its head?"

Here's an example: One time I powder-coated a bunch of old saws with beat-up wooden handles. I removed the saws, coated the metal saw blades in hot pink and yellow paint, reattached the handles, and hung the reinvented saws on the wall as a quirky art instal-lation. The juxtaposition of the old wooden handles and the bright paint colors was dynamite.

Another way to reinvent what you have and create an installation of sorts is to roam around your house and collect like items. If you have a globe in one room and a globe in another room and one in the garage, gather them up. Put them on display in one place to give them more impact. When you get sick of looking at it, move in something else. Keep your home fresh and alive—a rotating parade of things that light you up.

Navy Is the New Black

Color has the power to transport us. Navy blue nods to the ocean and nautical style, and it is rich and saturated enough to masquerade as black. Use this poser of a color in place of black to bring on that Pacific panache.

These are my fave navy tones, all by Benjamin Moore and Farrow & Ball.

Hale Navy
HC-154

Midnight
2131-20

Polo Blue
2062-10

Hague Blue
No. 30

don't forget nature

In your blind joy to go bold with color or deck out your stairwell with a two-story movie quote, don't nix the natural elements. All these surf-style details come together harmoniously when they're balanced with things you see in nature, like wood and plants. Choosing lighter-toned woods for hardwood floors or cabinets will keep it beachy and fresh. And when it comes to plants, make it your mission to have at least one green plant in every room. It perks up a space like nobody's business.

surf and turf

If you want to bring surf style to your mountain, country, or otherwise land-locked home but it's just not fitting in, there's a hack for that. Try wrapping surfboards in rope to dress them up for the location, and suddenly they're the star of the show.

Instead of surf flags in your mountain house, go for a mountaineer or ski theme with the flag subject matter.

And remember, if you're landlocked, skateboards are the new surfboards. Skateboard installations can fill up a whole wall and will instantly take you back to that California surf culture.

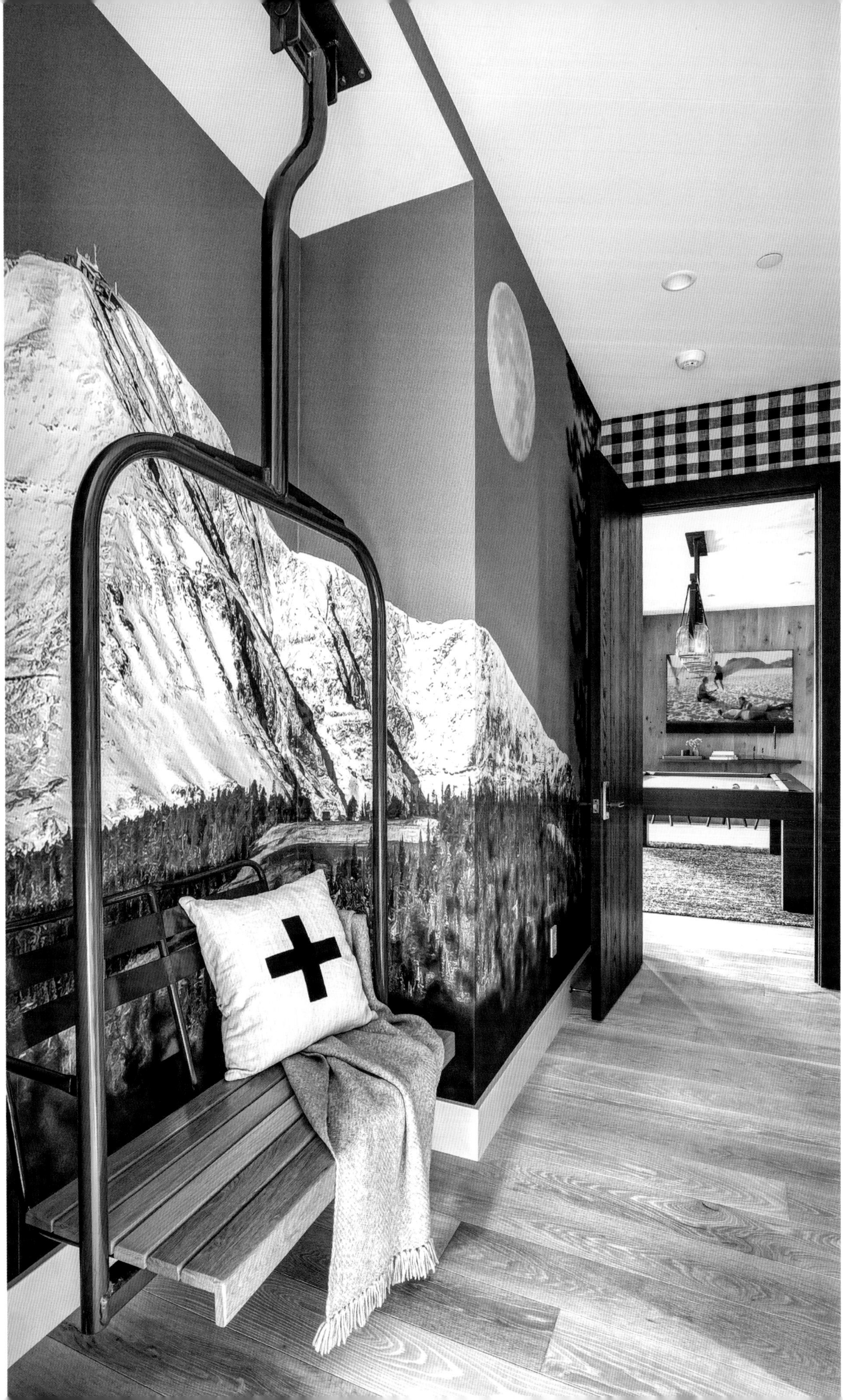

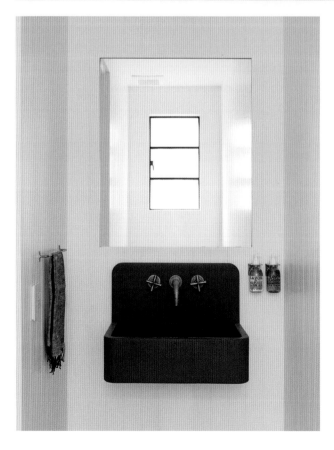

take a risk

I challenge you to take everything you learned in this book and really go for it with at least one idea. I've taught you how to surf, now it's your turn to paddle out and catch one. Go put your favorite song lyric up on a twelve-foot wall. Paint a big stripe all the way through your kids' bedroom. Put a massive tree in the middle of a window in your dining space. Wrap anything you can in rope. Paint polka dots on your bathroom wall. Put hooks on your wall and display toys like swim fins, goggles, or snorkels. Wallpaper a ceiling. Blow up your favorite photo to five feet by five feet and hang it on a big blank wall. Put a vinyl decal that says "Hello" on your Dutch-door window or display your favorite joke on your bathroom mirror. Line a wall with a giant photo mural of your favorite place. Coat your piano in bright yellow paint.

AMIGOS

Acknowl-edgments

The whole process of how this book came to be started with an email asking me if I wanted to make a book. My first reaction after receiving that email from Juree Sondker, my editor at Gibbs Smith, was, "I am so excited. I am so petrified." Juree, thank you for calming me down and believing in my ability to do something I never even dreamed I could do. My next step was to call my writer, Kelli Kehler, who basically was my brain, my director, my manager and now I get to call her my friend. Kelli, your talents are so grand. You took my eighth-grade surfer-boy vocabulary and wrote me a book!

Max Humphrey, you were my next call. "HELP! What should I do? I'm scared. I'm not sure I can do this." He basically said, "Enough . . . get to work. You'll never regret making a book."

Throughout my career in the surf industry, I glommed on early to the master creatives at Quiksilver: Steve Jones, Randy Hild, and one of my besties, Dana Marron. To me, they had the best style on the planet. I followed them shopping, traveling, and choosing restaurants that looked cool. This is how I got my "surf style."

My design team—well, you know how I feel about you. Nina and Kerry, we are going on a decade working together and the journey with you two has been nothing short of an awesome adventure. Hayley, Payton, Brooke, Katie, and RYAN, thank you for taking on all the challenges, random as they might be, to create our designs.

To the creatives I get to bring these projects to life with, photographers David Tsay, Karyn Millet, Ryan Garvin, Chad Mellon, Rebecca Tilley, Chad Mellon, Ezequiel Hurtado, Tanveer Badal, Lisa Romerein, Laurey Glenn, Gabe Sullivan, Doug Burke, Christopher Testani, Val Vogt, Molly Rose, Taylor Cole, Matt Sartain and Meilani Cottrell: You guys all blow me away with creating such beauty with your art. And I simply cannot forget my stylists who bring all the fun to the shoots, Merissa Libby, Erik Staalberg, and Michael Walters. THANK YOU for bringing it!

I am beyond grateful for the crew at Gibbs Smith. Juree, Ryan and Virginia, you guys have been the best and most excited collaborators on this project. I've loved working with this special, boutique publisher from the word GO.

OK family, now it's your turn. Tears are welling up as I write how your support, love, and encouragement have taken me through life with utter joy. Ryan, seriously, how did I land you as a husband? You are (get ready, this is cheesy) the wind beneath my wings! Calyn, Wyatt, and Rees, I live for you three. There are really no words to describe my love for you and how you've shaped my life and career. Thank you for spreading your love of surfing and the ocean throughout our family to further inspire this fun book.

photography credits

Jeffrey Allee: 9, 25, 222

Matt Allen: 216, 217

Tanveer Badal: 45 top and bottom right, 88 top, 127 right, 135, 149 bottom

Doug Burke: 124, 199

Raili Clasen: 56 middle top, 117

Taylor Cole: 102 bottom

Meilani Cottrell: 79 bottom right, 87 top left, 143, 175 bottom, 207 bottom

Jeff Divine: 38, 39, 90, 91

Baldemar Fierro: 224 bottom

Ryan Garvin: 14, 34 bottom, 36 middle, 36 right, 40, 41, 42, 61 top, 62, 63, 88 bottom, 108 left, 110, 113 bottom right, 114, 115, 118, 125 left, 126, 127 left, 130, 138, 141, 149 top right, 164, 165 left, 165 top right, 172, 175 top, 190 bottom, 194 left, 207 top, 208, 213 right

Laurey Glenn: 51, 54, 65, 67, 68, 69, 146 right, 147 left, 167

LeRoy Grannis Collection, LLC: 52, 53, 220

Ezequiel Hurtado: 24 left, 32, 46, 47, 92, 93, 168, 169

Chad Mellon: 19, 20, 21, 33, 87 bottom, 113 bottom left, 119, 165 bottom right, 184

Dick Metz Collection/SHACC: 218, 219

Karyn Millet: 23 (top), 24 right, 28, 34 top, 35, 36 left, 44 left, 45 bottom left, 48 bottom, 49, 55, 61 bottom, 64 bottom left, 64 middle and bottom right, 76 bottom, 79 left, 80, 81, 84 top right and left, 86, 87 top right, 96, 98, 99, 101, 102 top, 103, 104, 105, 106 top, 107, 108 top right, 112, 113 middle and top, 120, 122 top right, 122 bottom, 125 right, 128, 129, 131, 132, 133 right, 140, 146 left, 148, 149 top left, 151, 152, 153, 157, 161, 163 top, 170 right, 173, 178, 181, 185, 186, 188, 190 top right and left, 192, 194 right, 195, 206, 209, 212, 213 left, 215 top

Mike Moir: 137

Dewey Nicks: 13

Lisa Romerein: 18, 48 top, 64 top left, 111, 142, 150, 160, 179

Molly Rose: 109, 147 right, 174, 182, 183

Matt Sartain: 79 top right Ron Stoner/SHACC: 6, 73

Gabe Sullivan: 56 left, 56 right bottom, 58, 59, 64 top right, 70, 71, top 76, 89, 163 bottom, 171, 200, 201, 202, 203, 214

Christopher Testani: 139

Rebecca Tilley: 16, 23 bottom, 56 top right, 106 bottom, 155, 162, 166

David Tsay: 10, 22, 26, 27, 29 all, 31, 44 middle, 57, 60, 64 middle left, 64 very bottom, 66, 74, 75, 78, 82, 83, 84 bottom, 95, 97, 100, 108 bottom right, 121, 122 top left, 123, 133 left, 134, 144, 145, 154, 158, 165 middle right, 170 left, 177, 180, 187, 189, 190 middle, 191, 193, 196, 197, 204, 205, 210, 211, 215 bottom

Val Vogt: 77, 85, 224 top

about the authors

Raili Clasen stumbled into the interior design industry when her designer moved out of the country and she decided to try her hand at designing her own home. The finished result landed her in several magazines aiming to show readers how to capture Raili's California eclectic surf style. Early origins at Raisins Swimwear and then California-cool brands like Quiksilver, Roxy, Paul Frank and Alice Supply Co. left lasting impressions on Raili, forging a signature, no-rules style that has been described as "design with a wink." Raili now leads a full-service interior design team in Southern California that takes on projects ranging from funky 1920s beach cottages, to new construction at the Yellowstone Club, and Kelly Slater's famous Surf Ranch. Her work has been featured on TV shows including HBO Max's *Beach Cottage Chronicles* and Chip and Joanna Gaines' Magnolia Network series *Point of View: A Designer Profile Show*. In print, Raili's fun and inviting projects have appeared in *Architectural Digest, House Beautiful, Dwell, Coastal Living, Domino*, and more. Find her on Instagram at @railiclasen.

Kelli Kehler is a writer, editor, stylist, and book project manager. She started her career in journalism and later worked many years for beloved interior design blog *Design*Sponge*. She managed production of *In the Company of Women* and *Collective Wisdom*, was senior editor of *Good Company Magazine*, and was a writer for several lifestyle books from various publishers, including *House Story* and *Old Brand New*. Kelli lives in Southern California with her husband and two daughters. Find her on Instagram at @kellikehler.